Personal
Safety

Wise Guides

Personal Safety

Anita Naik

Illustrated by
Martin Remphry

Hodder
Children's
Books

a division of Hodder Headline Limited

For Joe

© Hodder Children's Books 2005

Published in Great Britain in 2005
by Hodder Children's Books

Editor: Hayley Leach
Design by Fiona Webb
Cover design: Hodder Children's Books

The right of Anita Naik to be identified as the author of the work
has been asserted by her in accordance with the Copyright, Designs
and Patents Act 1988.

10 9 8 7 6 5 4 3 2

ISBN: 0340884363

Printed by Bookmarque Ltd, Croydon, Surrey

The paper and board used in this paperback by Hodder Children's Books
are natural recyclable products made from wood grown in sustainable
forests. The manufacturing processes conform to the environmental
regulations of the country of origin.

Hodder Children's Books
a division of Hodder Headline Limited
338 Euston Road
London NW1 3BH

Contents

Acknowledgements

With grateful thanks to all of the following: Joseph Rattigan for all his advice on how to combat fear, and how to stay safe on the streets. Helen Prangnell for all additional research. Vicky Prior at AOL for Internet safety information and Anne Clark at Hodder Children's Books for her support.

Introduction

What's your view of the world? Do you feel scared to venture forth? Are you worried about being alone? Or are you someone who isn't at all anxious about crime, and would happily do anything and be anywhere for a bit of excitement? Perhaps you're someone who even thinks that reports of crimes against teenagers and children are exaggerated, or maybe you just can't be bothered to think about what might or might not happen because there are just too many other things going on in your life.

If so, it's worth considering some statistics, not to scare the pants off you, but to make you aware that personal safety is an issue for anyone who plans on having a life outside of their bedroom!

1. 25% of teenagers have been a victim of crime.
2. 50% of teen victims have suffered a violent crime.
3. 30% of teen victims have never reported the crime to anyone.

(SOURCE: VICTIM SUPPORT)

Of course, you may think none of the above is ever going to happen to you so you take the odd risk. You decide to take the short cut through the park alone at night, or you chat away on your mobile near a station (the number one place to be mugged). You think you'll be fine and hopefully you're right, but it's good to know how to look after yourself simply because it stops you from becoming someone who panics in the face of danger.

If, on the other hand, you often feel frightened of people you don't know and afraid of situations that are unknown to you, you need to figure out how to put these issues into perspective. In this way you'll know what to do when faced with a person or a group that bullies and intimidates you in the future.

Personal safety isn't about wrapping yourself in cotton wool and looking over your shoulder every five seconds, it's about learning to make rational decisions that help to keep you safe. If you want to feel confident, assured and secure when you're out and about, this guide can help. Work your way through the information inside and you'll not only increase your awareness and focus your ability to gauge risk; but you'll also know exactly what to do should the worst ever occur to you, someone you're with or a stranger on the street.

CHAPTER ONE

Why bother with safety?

Are you sick to death of being interrogated by your parents every time you go out, with questions such as: Where are you going? What time will you be back? Who are you going out with? What are you going to do? If so, like lots of teenagers, the idea of other people being worried about your safety isn't at the forefront of your mind. After all, your parents are only asking to annoy you/be nosy/spy on you – right? They couldn't possibly be the teeniest bit worried that you might get into trouble or danger could they? Do you think you're able to look after yourself and that they are treating you like a child? Well it's probably time to think again.

The truth is, when it comes to staying safe most people never give it a moment's thought until something scary happens to them or a person they know. While this attitude is probably better than hiding in your room all day because you feel too scared to venture out, the reality is, it pays to think about personal safety issues. Not so you can scare yourself senseless when you're out, but so you have it in your head to know what to do or say should the worst ever sneak up on you.

"My parents go on and on with the 'where are you? what are you doing?' questions, it's like they think I am going to go out and rob a bank or something"

TASHA, 14

"I always feel like my mum is spying on me. Sometimes she even calls me at my mate's house to check up on where I am. It's really embarrassing and just makes me switch off my phone and ignore her totally."

LEE, 13

"I'm not worried about safety – why should I be? That stuff in the papers is exaggerated and I have the sense not to do something stupid like get in a strange bloke's car, so I'm safe."

JOANNE, 14

Of course, like many people you may think you know what you'd do in a crisis, maybe hit someone back, shout loudly for help, or even feign a fainting attack. If so, consider what you'd do if something happened right this second; don't stop to think just write down your immediate reaction to these questions:

1. *What would you do if someone threatened you for no reason at the bus stop?*
2. *What would you do if you felt scared walking home at night?*
3. *Who would you tell if someone sent you an email that you felt threatened or scared by?*
4. *What would you do if you received a series of threatening text messages at school?*
5. *How many strangers would you trust automatically, if so why? (If you can't think of anyone, how about policemen, teachers, priests or people who ring your doorbell like the postman).*

If some of these situations sound ridiculous to you
and unlikely to happen, you should consider that
they are all incidents which have happened to
someone else, and probably to someone you know.

Look back over your answers and see how many
responses would help get you out of immediate
danger, and how many answers you can honestly
say you responded to quickly?

The answers should be:

1. *Move away instantly to a place of safety (a shop or a
   crowd of older people).*
2. *Go somewhere safe (a shop, café, bus station) and
   call someone to come and get you.*
3. *Your parents or a teacher.*
4. *Tell a teacher you trust and contact your mobile
   phone supplier for help.*
5. *You should never trust anyone automatically
   because people are not always what they seem.
   Even when policemen and official-looking people
   try to gain access to your home (i.e. people who
   say they are from the water board or gas company).
   Always ask for ID and if you still feel weird about
   them, ask them to come back later when someone
   else is about.*

What is personal safety?

"It's about doing all those things your parents yell at you about – like never walking home alone, and never trusting strangers."

SAMMI, 14

"It's about being sensible and not taking stupid risks"

PAUL, 14

Personal safety is not about never stepping out of your house and into the real world by yourself. Neither is it about letting adults frighten you into thinking the world is a bad place where you can't cope alone. Personal safety is about knowing how to deal confidently with, and hopefully avoid, the elements in society that we'd all rather weren't there, such as:

- The bullies on the street who pick on people weaker and smaller than themselves.
- The kids at school who get their kicks making other people miserable.
- The people on the Internet who pretend to be something they're not just to pull you in.
- And the people you meet in everyday life, who make you feel intimidated, persecuted and afraid, when all you're trying to do is go out and live your life.

It's also about feeling you can cope when:

- Something you never thought could happen suddenly happens to you.
- You, or someone you know, is getting hurt.
- A situation spirals out of control and turns violent.
- You get that feeling that you need help and need it fast.

Most importantly of all, personal safety is about forethought and using your common sense i.e. looking before you take that leap. Contrary to what you might think, people who are sussed about personal safety aren't wimps but they are people who have the sense to know how to look after themselves.

Consider your personal safety and you're guaranteed to:

- Feel more confident when you're out and about.
- Feel less scared when confronted by people behaving strangely.
- Be less likely to find yourself in a dangerous situation.
- Be more able to help friends and loved ones who find themselves in trouble.
- Be more able to keep away from trouble.

Could you protect yourself?

"Yes, I could. If someone tried to grab me I'd just kick them in the balls"

SUSAN, 14

"I may be small for my age but I am not afraid to fight someone who comes at me."

TONY, 13

"My mum says the best action to protect yourself is to scream loudly and run."

SAMMI, 14

"Yes, I can fight back. I'm as hard as the next bloke."

JACK, 13

Protecting yourself doesn't necessarily mean knowing how to attack someone who's attacking you. This may sound like a good idea in theory, but statistics show it's an excellent way to get hurt and make a situation worse. Though in the worst case scenario you may have no option but to fight (see page 81), bear in mind that shock does amazing things to our minds and bodies and can often immobilise the fastest and smartest of us. Don't automatically think you'll know how to fight back, because you probably won't. So it can help to have a range of options to choose from, such as:

- Knowing how to respond if someone grabs you.
- Knowing who to go to for confidential help.
- Knowing how to deal with the sense of panic that can immobilise you when you're scared.
- Knowing who to tell if someone's threatening you via text or email.
- Knowing what to do when walking down the street in the dark.

- Knowing how to avoid getting robbed or mugged.
- Knowing who to steer clear of on public transport.
- Knowing who to talk to online.

Being prepared may sound like a scary idea, but giving yourself a list of ideas to act on will equip you with an inner strength and a good dollop of confidence that will enable you to cope with anything and anyone you come across.

Facing reality (but not letting it freak you out)

"My parents are always saying watch out for this and that. They just do it to scare me so I do what they say. I don't really believe that kind of stuff happens."

MANDI, 13

"I read it's the people you know who are most likely to attack you. That's a kind of scary thought because it means who can you trust?"

SIAN, 14

"I don't trust anyone I don't know – that way I know I'll always be safe."

LEE, 14

Everyone's fear has a different face. Some people are afraid of spiders, others of the dark and others of flying. The fact is, fear is a natural response when we find ourselves in a situation that feels uncomfortable. Being sussed about your safety won't take this feeling away because fear is the body's internal alarm warning you that something is very wrong and you need to take some form of action.

If you're scared of looking afraid and you go against your gut feeling because you're worried about losing face or appearing a coward, be very careful because this kind of thinking can put you in danger. The key is to reassure yourself that everyone gets scared and frightened (ask the bravest person you know if they ever feel scared and their answer will be 'Yes'). It takes courage to admit you're afraid of certain things. Facing reality like this doesn't make the world a more frightening place; it just makes your options clearer.

For instance, accepting that walking through a dark park is dangerous because it's the perfect place for nutters to grab you isn't frightening but enlightening. It means you can now decisively take alternative action and choose to walk another way home. Likewise, knowing that there are people who go online and try to 'groom' young people (see chapter 5)

doesn't mean you should never go online, but that you should never give your personal details out to anyone you don't know. Even if you've swapped emails for months it still doesn't mean you actually know that person and you should never agree to meet them.

Who should you trust?

"I trust my best mate and no-one else. Not even my parents or my brothers."

MATT, 13

"I'd trust anyone in a uniform – because they are trained to look after people."

LISA, 12

Trust is a personal issue. It usually comes from a gut feeling deep down inside, and is almost instinctive. Contrary to what some people might think, it's rare to instantly trust someone before you know them because trust comes from observing and experiencing situations and seeing how people react to them.

Think of your best friend, you probably liked them on face value, but didn't really trust them until they proved their worth to you in some way. Trust comes with time, and that means it comes with getting to know someone, bit by bit and in person.

The fact is, attackers, muggers and people just looking for trouble, can come in all shapes, sizes and sexes. An attacker can be a young, good-looking man or woman, an older person and even someone younger, so it pays to remember it's not always the dodgy, weird-looking guy who might try something.

If you're unsure how much you can trust someone ask yourself:

- What three reasons make this person worthy of my trust?
- Does this person have my best interests at heart?
- Does this person look after his or her own safety (people who are reckless with themselves, tend to be reckless with others)?

- Has this person ever let me down badly?
- Has he or she let someone else down?
- Would I trust them to hold my diary without sneaking a look?

Keep your fear (and your parents' fear) in perspective

"Once I got so scared when I read the papers. I read about a girl who was kidnapped on the way to school and didn't see her family again for ten years. I was terrified that would happen to me and cried every night for two weeks until my mum heard me one night. She came in to my room and pointed out it was unlikely and rare and that's why it made the news and I didn't have to be scared. It was surprising how much talking to her helped me get it in perspective."

JENNI, 15

"My best mate got mugged for his mobile phone on the way home from school and now my parents won't let me use a mobile or take my CD Walkman to school. I think they're blowing things out of proportion."

JUSTIN, 14

Read the papers and it's easy to see why adults get hysterical and worried about stranger danger, weirdos lurking on the Internet and people who might mindlessly attack you. No wonder they get jumpy, try to overprotect you and scare you into staying safe. However, letting their fear dictate what you do will leave you frustrated and more likely to break their rules at the next opportunity. The smart compromise is to have a mutual set of safety measures in place that:

1. Make your parents feel assured that you are safe and being safe.
2. Maintain your new-found independence and don't swamp you.
3. Are realistic and workable in your every day life.

To find this common ground, sit down with your parents and work out a plan that incorporates these measures and makes you both happy. Remember a compromise is getting to a place where both parties have given a little, not where you get your own way.

The following are points you should try and come to an agreement over:

1. The time you have to be at home by – on school nights and weekends.
2. A promise that you will definitely call if you're in trouble no matter how angry you think your parents may be and no matter what time it is.
3. A set of ground rules for where you can and cannot go (if you disagree, work out why you're disagreeing. Is it because you're angry about

being told what to do, or are you upset because
you know it's an okay place to go?)

4. An agreement that you will tell them where you
   are and who you're with (that's honestly tell
   them where you are and who you're with) in
   exchange for them not checking up on you
   every ten minutes.

5. A check-in time when
   you're out – via text – with
   your mum (see chapter 5).

6. An agreement that you will
   call if you're running late so
   they don't sit around
   worrying about you.

7. A commitment that you
   won't break any of these
   points through lack of
   thought.

8. A promise that they trust you to make sensible
   decisions and not do anything reckless or risky.

To keep your fear levels in perspective, it's worth
keeping in mind that nearly all dangerous situations
can be avoided by keeping alert and making sensible
decisions. If in doubt about any of your decisions or
if your fears have spiralled out of control always
talk over your worries with one of the following:

• An adult you know and trust, like a parent,
  relative, or counsellor (see Resources page 97
  for who to talk to confidentially).

- Your best friend – if they really are your best friend, they'll want to keep you safe.
- An older sibling.
- Your GP – and ask them to keep it confidential.
- A friend's mother or father.

Risk taking – what is risky behaviour?

The real cornerstone of personal safety is knowing that keeping yourself safe is mainly about not taking unnecessary risks for the thrill of it. This means not doing something simply because you know it will get a positive reaction from your friends, or because they have pushed you into it.

Always think before you make decisions. It all may seem like a bit of fun to you but what are the real consequences of the action you're about to take? Ask yourself whether it will:

- Hurt you?
- Hurt someone else?
- Damage someone's property?
- Put you at risk of harm?

Remember, you can stay out of dangerous situations by being aware of what's going on, and alert to what's happening around you. Don't wander through life in a waking sleep: not thinking about

your actions, not noticing
that someone is about to
grab your phone trip
you up or even steal your
purse until it's too late. If
something you say or do
feels risky, the
likelihood is that it is
risky. Risky behaviour is:

- Lying about where you're going.

- Not telling anyone when you leave a place on your own (or with a stranger).

- Not having money or a phone on you in case of emergencies.

- Trusting people you don't know just because you think they look trustworthy.

- Doing something that feels stupid for a dare.

- Not looking out for your friends.

- Doing something that you know your parents would definitely disapprove of.

- Knowingly breaking the law.

- Lying to protect someone who you know is in a risky situation.

It always pays to be open about what you're doing. Of course, you don't always want your parents to know the truth and everyone is entitled to their own privacy. However, be smart and work out what should remain private and what shouldn't.
If in doubt imagine if you were a parent, what would you do in their situation (be honest with yourself)? That should give you the answer you need.

CHAPTER TWO

Awareness

"Ever since my brother was mugged on the train by three boys for his mobile I have learnt not to use mine out in the open or flash it about. It even makes me nervous when my friends talk loudly on theirs or they start texting in front of people. I am always telling them to be careful because it could happen to them as well."

CHARLIE, 15

Awareness is your biggest tool in keeping safe because if you can notice things going on around you nine times out of ten you can avoid all trouble. The problem is you may think you're an aware kind of person, but how much do you really notice when you're walking down the street? Are you so caught up in a conversation on your mobile or madly texting a friend that you never notice there is trouble ahead? Not sure how you score on the awareness scale? Then try this quick quiz:

1. Describe the sex, height and build of the last stranger you sat next to on the bus?

    A. You can't remember.
    B. You think you remember the sex of the stranger but you can't remember anything else.
    C. You think you would recognise them if you saw them again.

2. Did you notice who stood behind you the last time you were in a shop queue?

    A. You never looked round.
    B. You vaguely saw them as you walked away.
    C. It was definitely a man/woman and you're fairly sure you remember their height and hair colour.

3. A stranger suddenly speaks to you on the street? You...

    A. Are shocked because you didn't even notice them coming up to you.
    B. Saw them coming and wondered what they were going to say.
    C. Took a step back and faced them, ready for what they were about to say.

4. A friend says you walked right past her on the street. This...

A. *Happens to you a lot.*
B. *You only realised what happened as you walked off.*
C. *You saw her but you were actually trying to avoid her.*

5. *When walking down the street, you…*

A. *Are either listening to music or on your mobile phone.*
B. *Are talking to friends.*
C. *Are always in a rush but you stay alert.*

6. *When you do practise being aware you feel…*

A. *Nervous and anxious.*
B. *Like a spy.*
C. *More confident.*

Scores

Mostly As – The Waking Sleeper

You need an awareness wake up call. It's fine to wander around in what experts call a 'waking sleep' if you have someone with you, but wandering around in your own little world, means you are not looking after yourself or noticing when potential danger (such as having your mobile stolen) is near. Don't drift off into your private fantasy land and pay more attention to what's happening around you.

Mostly Bs – The Day Dreamer

You think you're more aware than you actually are. This is dangerous because you're living under a false sense of security. If something happened you'd actually be a weak witness because you only *think* you noticed what was going on. Focus on the present moment and look at what's happening around you.

Mostly Cs – The Awareness Expert

You're super aware of life and that's brilliant. What's more you have the sense to know that noticing what's going on around you doesn't make you paranoid or afraid, but more confident and assured as you walk down the street.

What is awareness and how can you get some?

Learning to be aware is easier than you think. It's about living consciously in the moment but not suspiciously glancing over your shoulder every five seconds. People with good awareness skills, can spot a potentially hazardous situation a mile off, then judge what's going on and work out the fastest way to avoid it.

The best way to increase your awareness is to set yourself awareness tasks every day so you train your mind into recalling and noticing things automatically. It's important that you keep up the momentum – do it every day until it becomes second nature to you.

To help train your mind, start by making yourself spot three things on the way to school, and three things on the way home every day. For instance:

1. Who stood next to you in the bus queue? What were they wearing, were they male or female, and how old were they?
2. What was the colour and make of the car sitting outside your house as you left that morning (not the car belonging to your parents)?
3. Who stood out on the bus, train or walk to school and why?

The next step is, knowing what to do when you've noticed something unsettling. To help yourself come up with realistic options, run through some of the following potential scenarios with your friends and think of ideas about what you would do if:

1. You see a bunch of rowdy and drunk boys walking towards you.

    Good idea: Cross to the other side of the street or take a wide berth around them.
    Bad idea: Walk straight through them.

2. Someone walks too close to you on the street.

    Good idea: Stop in your tracks, turn around and start walking the other way.
    Bad idea: Walk faster.

3. You realise the person next to you on the bus is touching your leg on purpose.

    Good idea: Get up and move.
    Bad idea: Stay where you are for fear you might be wrong.

4. You notice that the people behind you at the cinema have started a fight.

    Good idea: Move away.
    Bad idea: Turn round and watch them.

The more you discuss ideas and situations like these, the more confident you'll feel about automatically acting on your awareness skills and placing yourself well out of the path of trouble.

Fear and anxiety

"All this talk about being aware just makes me feel anxious about who's going to attack me or try something on. I now feel really nervous when I walk down the street or am sitting alone on the bus. At least before I never even thought about it."

EMMA, 15

"Sometimes I get really scared when I see trouble happening, I become all sweaty and hot. I hate feeling like this – it makes me feel like a coward".

JAKE, 13

Of course, when you first start becoming more aware, it does bring to mind all the horrible things that could happen. However, personal safety is also about keeping your fear in perspective. Being aware doesn't mean living in permanent fear, neither does it mean walking around as if the next stranger you meet will attack you. Remember it's normal to feel anxious but it's not normal to feel fearful all the time.

If you feel scared and can't put it down to anything in particular it's likely you're focusing on the downside of awareness. Remind yourself that you're keeping your eyes open to boost your confidence and your ability to judge what's happening around you, not because you're about to be attacked. If you feel so afraid that you're worried you can't be on your own, you need to talk to someone – your parents, or an adult you trust – and allow them to put your fears into perspective.

Understanding fear

To keep your fear from overwhelming you it helps to understand why fear happens and how it affects your body. The fear you feel when something scary happens such as watching a horror film or if you're in a confrontation is actually your body releasing adrenaline.

Adrenaline is a hormone released by the brain in response to a stressful situation. It increases the heart rate and raises blood pressure – making you feel hot, sweaty and ready to run or fight.

When it swamps the body it charges you and makes you stronger, faster and even gives your body the ability to absorb more pain than it normally would. An adrenaline response is directly linked to our distant past when danger and death were more likely and we needed adrenaline to either fight or run for our lives. Today it is known as 'fight or flight' but it is a strange sensation since in most cases we neither need to fight or escape.

Think of being in an exam room, when you can't answer a question on the paper and you feel hot, sweaty and panicked. You are experiencing the 'fight or flight' response. The important thing to realise is:

1. Everybody feels fear and gets a rush of adrenaline when scared. Feeling like this is perfectly natural and does not make you a coward.
2. People often freeze when their body releases adrenaline quickly because they are not used to the feeling and mistake it for panic.
3. Adrenaline is there to help you not hinder you, but you need to utilise it quickly by taking action.

The purpose of adrenaline

Slow release adrenaline when you're thinking about a scary forthcoming event

If you know something scary is on its way such as an exam, an argument with your best friend or even a sporting event, your body will release small amounts of adrenaline over a period of days as the deadline for the event approaches. Your body does this to help you take action and either avoid the event or face it sensibly.

Adrenaline release due to thinking about what may or may not happen

Adrenaline is released if you think about the potential consequences of a scary event such as what you'll say to a bully or how you'll do in an exam. This has its uses – as the fear of the possible outcome helps you work out how you're going to tackle things.

Quick adrenaline release at the point of confrontation

This is known as an adrenaline dump, when a large quantity of adrenaline is instantly released into the body as a result of an immediate or unexpected threat. This is the most common adrenaline release in a street attack and is the most likely to cause you to freeze, but is also very powerful. It helps your mind to see that you're in instant danger and helps you to take immediate action.

Slow adrenaline released after the confrontation

After a confrontation, the consequences of the confrontation will go through your mind. A slow trickle of adrenaline will be released so that you can deal with what might happen next e.g. what if you fail that test, or the police get involved in the fight you were just in, or your parents find out you skipped school. This is important because it helps you to seek and ask for help.

Adrenaline released in a combination

A combination of all these types of adrenaline may happen over one incident. For instance:

1. You may walk home daily on a route where you know there is a potential troublemaker who does not like you and wants to confront you. This equals a slow adrenaline release over days so you can decide what action you're going to take.

2. On the way home one day that person confronts you – cue an immediate adrenaline dump that forces you to take action.
3. In the middle of the confrontation you see a friend of the troublemaker approach – you get another adrenaline dump as you consider what's going to happen now.
4. His friend takes the troublemaker away and threatens to come back if you tell anyone; you go home and think about this – adrenaline is released slowly to make you take action and tell someone what's happened.

Your body's response to adrenaline

It's worth knowing how adrenaline affects your body so you're not scared when you feel it sweeping through you. Adrenaline release will lead to:

1. Body or limbs shaking.
2. Palms of the hands becoming sweaty.
3. Mouth becoming dry.
4. Voice becoming high pitched or has a tremor.
5. Feeling physically sick.
6. Feeling a need to go to the toilet.
7. Tunnel vision.
8. Time distorting and events happening really quickly or very slowly.

9. Heart beating faster to supply blood to your muscles.
10. Feeling a rising sense of panic.

Your body has these responses in order to channel all its energy into helping you survive, while cutting off blood to non-essential functions which are not needed for instant survival. This is one reason why you may suddenly feel sick as blood is diverted away from your stomach.

Facing fear

Due to the dangers humans faced in the past the natural human instinct is to run rather than fight. We are taught all our lives that it is wrong to fight yet called cowards if we don't. Always ignore what you think you should do to save face and base your decisions solely on your safety. Remember, there is no shame in feeling like you want to run when you feel afraid; and it's usually the correct and safest thing to do.

Trusting your gut instinct

If you're unsure what fear feels like, or sometimes you get an odd feeling but you aren't sure if it's fear, it can help to learn to trust your gut instinct. This is the feeling that you get when something's not quite right. Maybe it will be a prickly feeling on your neck or a kind of ache just below the breastbone. Sometimes, your stomach may even flip over or you'll feel jittery and have the urge to move away really quickly. This is your gut warning you to be on your guard and to be ready to move because something is not right.

Of course it takes time to learn to trust your gut feeling, but if you've ever hit trouble and then thought, 'I knew that was going to happen' – it's a sure sign that your gut instinct is working and you should start listening to yourself. Things your gut feeling will react to:

- People who seem nice, but for some reason, you can't put your finger on what makes you feel uncomfortable when you are with them.
- Places that have an 'atmosphere'.
- Situations that seem heavy with tension.
- Other people getting jittery and scared.

Building confidence in yourself

Of course, learning to listen to your own voice over that of friends telling you everything's okay, or adults insisting things are fine is a tough one. It takes a fair bit of self-confidence to believe your feelings are right and to act on your gut instinct, instead of being pulled along by the crowd.

To boost belief in yourself:

1. Think of all the times you knew you were right but didn't say so until it was too late. For example, knowing the answer in class but being too afraid to say it. Or knowing a fight was going to happen but not moving until it had started.
2. Don't ask for someone's opinion in a situation that feels wrong, but instead state yours. For example don't say: 'Do you think he's odd?' but 'He's odd, let's go!'
3. Look at people's agendas. For example, why is your friend trying to get you to stay somewhere you feel uncomfortable in?
4. Learn to stand your ground. It doesn't matter if you're wrong, it's better to act on your gut feeling than wait to be proved right.

To boost belief in your physical abilities:

1. Get active. If you can't even walk upstairs without getting out of breath or you are overweight, you will never have faith in your physical abilities and you will always be at the mercy of stronger and fitter people than you.

2. Try to get fit in case you ever have to escape from a situation. You will need to be able to run and you may have to jump and even push people away.

3. Stamina is the most important thing you have to build as you may have to run for a long time and to deal with the energy drained by shock. Some of the best ways of gaining stamina are by going for regular runs or swims. It is best to do this with a friend for fun and extra protection.

4. You will also need a level of muscle strength for whatever physical obstacles you encounter, so do something you enjoy – tennis, yoga or circuit training.

5. Do this training in moderation and don't over-train. Ask your PE teacher for advice, or even work-out at home to a fitness video.

6. Get walking – it's one of the best forms of exercise and can be done anywhere and at anytime.

To boost belief in your mental abilities:

Build a personal fear pyramid – this is a list of your personal fears from one to ten, with one being your smallest anxiety and 10 being your biggest fear. For instance:

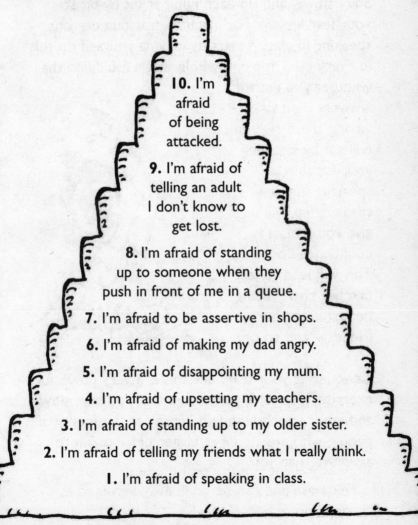

10. I'm afraid of being attacked.

9. I'm afraid of telling an adult I don't know to get lost.

8. I'm afraid of standing up to someone when they push in front of me in a queue.

7. I'm afraid to be assertive in shops.

6. I'm afraid of making my dad angry.

5. I'm afraid of disappointing my mum.

4. I'm afraid of upsetting my teachers.

3. I'm afraid of standing up to my older sister.

2. I'm afraid of telling my friends what I really think.

1. I'm afraid of speaking in class.

When you have your list you start at number one and work your way through them (your aim isn't obviously to get to your biggest fear but to increase your belief in what you're capable of facing).

Start slowly and do each number bit by bit so your fear lessens. For instance, fear number one – speaking in class – start by making yourself do this in every class, for one whole week. You'll find that whether you get the answers right or wrong, the thrill you will get by knowing your capable of speaking out and speaking up, will give you a massive confidence boost. This will lead to fear number two – being honest with your friends – and so on.

Conquering your fears like this is a very powerful exercise. It enables you to see that you have power and inner strength and you aren't at the mercy of people who are stronger, bigger, older or more assertive than you.

It's sense not bravado that keeps you safe

"I'm not afraid of anything. If someone comes up to me I won't feel bad about hitting them or too scared to yell at them. I'll take on anyone. I'm not a coward."

JACK, 14

"I always shout at people who get in my way it makes them respect me and treat me properly."

SHELLEY, 14

You may of course be strong, and fast and even smarter than most people but don't ever let this lull you into a false sense of security. Self-defence and personal safety are about avoidance rather than physical self-defence. Your key to self-protection is to be alert, aware and wary but not paranoid or aggressive.

As we've said earlier in this chapter, by becoming more aware, knowing what fear does to your body and having more belief in your abilities you can avoid most kinds of trouble. So forget bravado and putting on a show, your goal should always be to escape without injury and remain safe rather than win fights or make a show of someone.

CHAPTER THREE

How to gauge risk

As well as being alert and aware it's essential that you know how to gauge risk, because this will (1) help protect you and (2) help you make instant decisions which will keep you out of danger. The good news is you don't have to be a mind reader to see trouble coming, all you have to do is be adept at picking up clues in the actions and behaviour of the people around you.

"I can see trouble coming a mile off. My friends think I am paranoid but I've got them to steer clear of trouble makers many times."

LINDA, 16

"I think I'm okay at spotting trouble but now and again I have been caught out by some of the guys round here."

JOHN, 13

Clear clues that something is wrong when you're out and about are:

- A sudden change in a place's atmosphere.
- Silence or a sudden burst of noise.
- People moving backwards.
- People crossing over the street.
- Someone looking pointedly at you as they walk past.
- People shouting.
- Someone sounding panicked.
- Someone crying.

Clear clues that something is not right with a person you have just met:

- Not feeling their story is truthful.
- Spotting them get defensive when questioned further.
- Noticing that they turn questions on you to avoid answering your queries.
- They sound too good to be true.
- They ask you to keep something a secret.
- They try to turn you against someone you know very well.
- They over flatter you.

Clues that you're about to do something risky:

- You know your parents would be angry if they found out what you were doing.

- You keep it secret from certain friends as you know they'd put a downer on it.
- You feel uneasy about doing it.
- You're worried you might hurt yourself, damage something or get in trouble with the law.
- You know you're not supposed to be doing it and that's the thrill.
- You feel an adrenaline surge at the thought of it.

It takes time to learn to pick up clues and read them. Help yourself by fine-tuning your private eye talents and set yourself the following tasks for the next five days to help build your risk gauging skills:

1. Make a note of how many times in one night you notice trouble about to happen when you're out with friends.
2. Write down the amount of times you chose not to do something risky this week i.e. walk home through a deserted park, use your phone late at night, take an unlicensed minicab, let a stranger buy you a coffee.
3. Note how many new people you came across who set off your gut instinct (think good and bad).
4. Note how many times you felt your friends did something risky.

Projecting confidence when you're out and about

The good news is that listening to your gut feeling, and being able to pick up clues from other people's behaviour, has a multitude of benefits beyond personal safety. For instance, being able to read someone and a situation effectively can help you in social situations, when you go to get a job and even at school. Roll these elements together with a talent for reading someone's body language and what you'll essentially do is boost your EQ (emotional intelligence) power.

Emotional intelligence is the way we use our emotions to interpret people's behaviour and make judgement calls. For instance, we meet a policeman in the street and we decide whether or not to trust them, based not on their uniform, but on how they speak to us, what  they actually say, their body language and the authority with which they speak. We use our EQ (as opposed to IQ) to interpret all this information and then make a decision based on that.

If you're shy and find it hard to talk to people it can be hard to project confidence effectively and this can make you look smaller and weaker than you are. Shyness is a form of self-consciousness and is linked to low self-esteem, so to beat it and start looking confident you have to regularly push the boundaries of your world.

Do something you're afraid of everyday, even if it's just expressing your opinion to a friend (see the Fear Pyramid in chapter 2).

To project confidence, the key is to fake it. Hold your head up, throw your shoulders back and walk tall to create a positive impression to others. Make eye contact when you listen to people and generally pretend to be more confident than you are. In time you'll forget you're even faking and actually become the confident person you appear to be.

Think about what you're wearing

To stay safe you need to keep all your senses sharp and this is one reason to think about what you're wearing. Apart from avoiding wearing headphones when you're out walking alone, be smart about what you've got on. Hoodies, for instance, block your peripheral vision, as do parkers with hoods, and umbrellas pulled down close to the body. For girls high heels may look great, but are they easy to run in? Undone trainers may look trendy but can

you leg it in them
if you have too?
Finally, with skirts
and trousers can you
walk briskly in them
if need be or are
they too short and
tight, or too baggy
and loose? It sounds
ridiculous to think
about your clothes
in this way but it's
always a factor
worth considering
when you're getting
dressed for a night out.

Confidence on the street

Most people looking to harass or confront people
will always look for someone who already looks
like a victim i.e. easy prey, rather than someone
who looks confident and therefore maybe too
much trouble for them to bother. To be the latter
kind of person always ensure you:

1. Walk with authority. Don't dawdle as you
   wander down a street, hold your head up and
   stride as you walk. Look like you know where
   you are going and where you are.

2. If you move quickly (rather than run, or look panicked as you walk) people are less likely to get in your way, grab you or even come up to you.

3. If you have to speak to a stranger for whatever reason (perhaps they have approached you for directions), look them in the eye and speak with confidence. Maintain a good distance between you, if they step forwards don't be afraid to ask them to keep back, or put your hands out to stop them encroaching on your personal space (this is the space that you feel comfortable talking to strangers in – see pages 50–52).

4. Don't walk with headphones on. Do walk facing traffic, and be aware of people acting suspiciously in your path or behind you.

Common sense when you're on the street

1. Always keep your valuables and mobile phones hidden from sight. Putting temptation on view can make you an unwitting target.

2. Place your bag with the opening facing inwards, towards you and your body. Bags with the strap going across your body are best as these are harder to grab. However, if someone does try to take your bag, always let it go and never fight for it, as you're more likely to get hurt while trying to keep hold of it.

3. Always tell someone where you are going before you leave.

4. If you're going somewhere new have a plan of your route before you leave, so you don't wander around looking lost.

5. If you are lost, go into a shop to use your mobile phone or ask in a shop for directions.

6. When walking, always walk in the middle of the pavement so that nobody can suddenly appear from doorways, alleys or cars.

7. Keep away from parked cars with engines running.

8. Walk wide around corners so that you have a clear view of the next road and you cannot be surprised.

9. Cross the road and avoid individuals or groups of people who make you feel uncomfortable on sight.

10. Avoid known trouble spots: areas with bad reputations.
11. Be aware of your surroundings and the people in them but do not stare. Staring at someone will, in many cases, beckon trouble.

Confidence at night

1. Always walk facing traffic so that you can see what is coming toward you.
2. If you have to use an unfamiliar or unlit route make note of possible escape routes and public places such as cafés and shops so that you know how to escape or get to a safe place quickly.
3. Try to keep at least one hand free at all times. Holding your keys in your hand can help you feel more secure so you can use it against someone in the worst case scenario (though remember your first thought should always be to run).
4. If you have a bag be prepared to throw it at an individual to make an escape.
5. Keep your keys separate from anything with your address on it.

Confidence on public transport

1. Even on public transport stay alert and aware of what is going on around you. Don't go upstairs

if the bus is empty or you can hear a racket happening above you.

2. Stay near an exit, other groups of passengers or, if you can, near a driver or guard. They may not be able to protect you but their presence should help deter people and they should be able to communicate with someone to get help.

3. Know the timetable of the public transport that you use so you do not have to wait a long time at bus stops alone.

4. Try to use stations and bus stops that are always busy.

5. Don't go through an underpass unless it's essential.

6. Stay in well-lit areas of stations.

7. Make sure that you know the time of your last train, tube or bus.

8. Don't talk about any personal details in public places or on public transport, especially anything that will include your home address or details of your movements.

9. If you can't keep your bag out of sight make sure it is close to you, preferably touching you, perhaps on your lap.

Of course there's no getting around it, there are weird people in this world and you may come across one of them when you're on a crowded bus or train. These are the type of people who get their kicks from touching you 'accidentally-on-purpose' when you're crammed up close to them in a rush hour crush. The way to deal with them, is:

1. Move away as soon as you can – if possible.
2. When it's not possible, don't be embarrassed to say very loudly, 'Get your hands off me', and look at them so everyone knows what they are doing.
3. Once you've said this, ask people to let you through so you can move away.
4. Tell the driver what has happened and stay near him or her.
5. When it's your stop, check to see this person doesn't try to get off with you. If they do, wait a few more stops and then phone someone to come and pick you up.

This may be embarrassing to say and do, but everyone around you will be sympathetic and the person who is doing it thinks you won't have the courage to shame them in public.

How to read body language signals

In gauging risk it helps if you can read someone's non-verbal messages. 55% of how we interpret others comes from body language so it's essential you know how to spot certain body signs.

Eye contact

With friends it's normal to keep eye contact when listening, and then maintain eye contact for about 2–3 seconds when talking (we all tend to look away and glance back as we're speaking). However, staring at someone for longer than 3 seconds comes across as aggressive and confrontational, as does not blinking and fixing a look on your face as you stare. If someone is staring at you, don't try to stare them out – they are being confrontational and trying to get a response out of you, so look away, and move away.

Smiling

A real smile is hard to fake because it turns up the corners of the eyes. Look in a mirror and smile naturally and watch how your face moves and looks. Now fake it. You'll see that the fake smile just doesn't reach the eyes. If someone smiles at you and you get the sense it's not real, the chances are you're right and you should be wary of their motives and agenda (what they may be trying to get you to do).

Tactile behaviour

Some people are more tactile – that's touchy-feely – than others. They tend to touch your arm or playfully push you when they speak. If you're not a touchy-feely person it's okay to reject these moves even from a friend. By simply moving back when they go to touch you, you're sending them the message that it isn't okay. Having said that, there are no-go areas of the body which people, especially strangers, shouldn't go to touch. These include:

- Your face
- Your hair
- Your breasts/groin/bottom
- Your waist

Again if someone goes for these areas, move away or just say 'No' and push their hands away.

Their stance

How someone stands in front of you is also a clear signal of their intentions. Standing full on, with legs apart is usually a confrontational and aggressive stance. Being jumpy and jittery while they talk to you i.e. fidgeting, means they are up to something and you should be wary. Towering over you as you sit or trying to pin you into a corner is also aggressive.

Controlling the distance between you and other people

An essential part of personal safety is being able to control the space between you and strangers. This is the distance you want a person to maintain while they are talking to you. Personal space varies from person to person and country to country. Some people are just useless at judging it and so can make you feel uncomfortable and threatened by coming too close.

To check what your personal space zone is, stand against a wall and get a good friend to slowly walk towards you. When they get too close (they are invading your space), you'll find that your hands will instinctively come up to stop them and you will move your body away.

Now, to discover your differing zones get someone you don't know very well (a friend of a friend) to do it again. This time work out your:

1. Comfort zone – the ideal distance where you prefer people to stand.
2. Feeling-a-bit-odd zone – the distance that rings your warning bells.
3. Feeling-threatened zone – the distance that freaks you out.
4. Move-back-now zone – the distance where you instinctively push someone away.

Knowing what your zones are can help you to spot if someone is about to invade your space, make you feel uncomfortable or corner you. Remember, you'll always let a friend closer than a stranger, so the second you feel odd about someone coming near don't be afraid to be assertive and:

1. Put your hands out as a warning to stop.
2. Take two steps back.
3. Ask them not to come closer.
4. Side step them (always move towards an open space not into a closed one).

Assertiveness v. aggression

There's a very big difference between being assertive and being aggressive which is why it pays to know the difference.

Assertiveness is direct and positive behaviour.
Aggression is hostile and destructive behaviour.

Assertive behaviour makes your position clear without inviting a negative response, whereas aggressive behaviour invites an aggressive response as well as letting the other person know they have well and truly rattled you. Avoid aggression at all costs simply because it pushes people over the edge and can accelerate what is already an explosive situation.

Examples of assertive and aggressive behaviour:

If a stranger steps into your personal space:

- An assertive response would be,
  'You're too close. Move back'.
- An aggressive response would be,
  'Get out of my face, NOW!'

If someone puts their hand on your arm:

- An assertive reaction would be to firmly
  move your arm away.
- An aggressive reaction would be to hit their
  hand away.

If a stranger asks you where you are going:

- An assertive response would be to say,
  'Sorry I don't speak to strangers'.
- An aggressive response would be to say,
  'F*** off'.

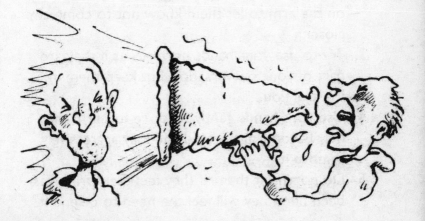

Avoiding confrontation

Now that you're aware of your own comfort space, bear in mind that the distance from which you can reach out and touch someone is also the space from which you can use your hands to push people away (if need be). While your primary objective with someone invading your space is always to get away from them, sometimes you may have to use other tactics if they have cornered you or they are being thick skinned about your warning signals.

Here's what to do:

1. Try not to touch them so as not to antagonise them. If someone does enter your space you can step to the side to avoid them. Though don't make this movement a statement (see body language, pages 48–50).
2. If they enter your space again, lightly touch them on the arm to let them know not to come any closer.
3. Try to use your hands normally as if they are part of your conversation, but keep them in front of you.
4. Use your hands gently. If you're too firm they may become aggravated and may aggressively remove it.
5. Do not insult them. If they feel their pride has been hurt they will feel the need to defend it.

6. If the person still comes close use your hand with more vigour, possibly using your palm to keep them at a distance once they make contact. Retract your hand to avoid it being grabbed.

7. If the person still comes forward underline your distance by making a forceful comment – 'Could you just stay there for a second'. Any dialogue you enter into should be laced with options to allow them to leave with their pride intact. Work on being a good actor (practise scenarios with your friends). The conversation you hold should be polite and confident but get more forceful as it continues.

8. Try to let other people know with your comments that the attention you are receiving is not wanted.

9. Say loudly – 'Please leave me alone!' This may make them feel ashamed or fearful that you have drawn attention to an adult harassing a child. And also alert people around you that you don't know this person and you need help.

Lessen your risk in risky situations

As scary as these scenarios are, you can avoid a physical confrontation by learning how to lessen your risk in a risky situation. The following five pointers are effective ways to get help when you're in trouble.

I. Don't be afraid to make a scene

Believe it or not, most of us are afraid of
embarrassment even in a potentially dangerous
situation, so we won't scream, rant and rave and
generally make the biggest fuss possible. However,
you need to make a scene, and a loud one, as the
more attention you bring to what's happening the
more likely your attacker will be to run off, and
the more likely someone will stop to help you. To
ensure that you're making yourself clear, tell people
what's happening and ask for help and keep asking
until someone comes.

2. Don't be afraid to shout at an adult

Most of us are taught to respect other adults,
especially the ones we know. However, being
attacked isn't the time to remember your manners.

If an adult is making scary advances at you, threatening you and coming at you don't be afraid to use your voice and tell them to stop. Do what you have to do to make your position clear and again be as loud as you can.

3. Ask for help

Don't think you're misjudging a situation – if you feel scared or threatened you're not imagining it. Ask for help from anyone around and ask for it immediately.

4. Never trust anyone to take you to another location

Don't trust anyone who makes you feel uncomfortable. Never ever let them take you to another location and don't fool yourself that keeping quiet will 'help' you. All these things work in their favour not yours. Act decisively and get away as quickly as possible.

5. Use all your strength

If you're going to try and push someone away do it with all your strength and don't be half-hearted about it. Be realistic though, you cannot fight someone twice your size and weight. Your aim should be to distract them and then escape.

CHAPTER FOUR

Keeping safe

"I don't feel unsafe in the summer – I only feel unsafe when it's dark outside and I am walking home alone"

SHEENA, 14

"If I was scared I think I'd run to the nearest house or a woman or couple on the street for help."

TIA, 13

"Once I was walking home late from school and it was quite dark. There wasn't anyone behind me but I suddenly felt scared and ended up taking this short cut across the park just to get home quicker. Afterwards I realised it was a really stupid thing to do – imagine if someone had been following me? I gave them the ideal opportunity to try something."

YASMINE, 15

Getting to safety

When you feel scared the most common reaction, like Yasmine is to feel, 'I've got to get home and get home now'. This is great if you're

five seconds from your front door but not so great
if getting home involves hanging around for a bus or
running home alone. If you feel unsafe you owe it
to yourself to instantly place yourself in a safer
environment (even if you feel a bit silly or worry
you might be over reacting). The way to do this is
to think in advance about some potential safe
places, so in your mind you always know instantly
where you'll head if you feel in trouble.

For most people, safe places are places where they
know they can trust someone such as:

- Their school.
- A friend's house.
- The police station.
- A relative's house.
- Home.

If these places aren't near, other places to opt
for are:

- A chemist (ask the pharmacist for help).
- A crowded café where you can ask the owner
  for help.
- The manned ticket hall of a train or bus station
  (ask a guard for help).
- A shop where you can see there is a security
  guard and plenty of people besides someone
  behind a counter.

- A house with a light on.
- A library or any other public place.

Places to avoid when scared:

- Running into parks or across common ground.
- Underpasses, railway sidings and overhead bridges.
- Any kind of shortcut or alleyway (even if you know it really well).
- Car parks and multi-storey car parks.
- Building sites or deserted houses.
- Anywhere very busy such as a take-away place where it's hard to get the attention of people working there.

As scary as some of these places may seem – the majority of adults will help you if you ask them too. When asking for help it's important not to let them make decisions for you or let them tell you you're imagining it (people think this is reassuring but always trust your own judgement first).

When asking for help:

- Tell them what you're scared of.
- Ask them to call someone for you (a parent or trusted adult).
- Wait in the shop or public place until you get help.
- Keep asking for help if they ignore you.
- Don't be embarrassed into thinking you're making a fuss (you're not).
- Don't persuade yourself you're being silly.
- Be clear about what help you want.

Looking strong on the street

"I am always being pushed about by older girls where I live, even when I am just going to the shops for my mum. I want to look tough but I think I look like someone you'd want to pick on. I'm small and look like I'd fall the minute you came near me."

LIZZIE, 13

"I just stare people out it makes them all stay away."

TOM, 14

Regardless of your size, it's good strong posture that is the key to looking confident on the street. If you can stand up straight, and walk with authority, you will appear taller and stronger no matter how small and slight you may be.

In an ideal world we would all have great posture, unfortunately thanks to comfy sofas, school desks and computers most of us spend our lives hunched over with our heads down. To improve your posture all you need to do is stand in front of a long mirror and take a good look at yourself. Are your shoulders rounded? Is your chin being held too high or too low (can you see the underside of your neck or the top of your head)? Is your stomach hanging out? Are you placing your body weight more on one hip than the other? If you answered 'yes' to any of these you need to work on your posture.

For good posture do the following:

1. Pull in your stomach – imagine your belly button pulling in towards your spine. However, don't pull it in so much that your ribs tighten and you can't breathe. If you do it right your stomach will suck upwards and you'll feel your back lengthen. A good way to remind yourself to do this is to get a piece of strong string, pull your belly button in and tie the string around your waist (so it's snug, rather than cutting into your skin). Now every time you let your stomach flop outwards the string will tighten and you'll be reminded to sit up properly.

2. Hold your head up – the head is the heaviest part of the body and if you don't work your neck muscles they literally become too weak to hold your head properly. Don't let your head slump forwards; imagine your chin tucking backwards (almost giving you a double chin). At the same time imagine a piece of string pulling you upwards from the top of your head. Do it right and you should feel instantly taller and longer.

3. Roll your shoulders back – most of us walk about with our shoulders round by our ears. For good posture you need to literally roll your shoulders back. Imagine your shoulder blades sliding down your back and your head moving away from your body (your neck should then automatically lengthen).

4. Stay relaxed – when you tell someone to stand up straight the first thing they usually do is suck in their stomach and puff out their chest. This is not only uncomfortable but also hard to maintain. Good posture should not be a strain, you should be pulled in but your body should be relaxed and loose. If you're not, loosen your arms and shake your head a bit and try again.

For good walking posture:

1. Practise walking with a book on your head. This works because it makes you automatically stand tall. Practise in your bedroom twice a day.
2. Walk with authority – this means walk, or rather stride, as if you're a person with a place to get to. Walking slowly and idly knocking into people and gazing into the far distance shows others that: (a) you're not paying attention to what's happening around you and (b) you're easy prey if they wanted to try something.

3. Don't be aggressive – it's easy to take confident walking too far and march off looking as if you want trouble. So again, be confident, but look assertive, not aggressive. Don't barge past people and don't make eye contact and scowl at people.

Boys beware

It's a sad fact of life that national crime statistics published by the Home Office show that when it comes to street crime, boys aged from ten to 17 are among the most vulnerable sections of society, more vulnerable than young girls and old people. Worse still, most of those who prey on boys tend to be the same age as their victims.

Figures from the Metropolitan Police area (London), where the problem is at its worst, show that 65 per cent of people accused of mugging and other street crime in London between April and November 2003 were between ten and 17 years of age. According to the Home Office, half of all victims involved in mobile phone theft nationally were boys aged 15 or 16.

The main problem is that we all walk around with lots of things that are worth stealing these days and the most likely items to be stolen are mobile phones and money. Threats, bullying, violence and intimidation are just some of the things you have to watch out for if you're out alone, or on your way home from school.

While the most helpful thing to do is to not to bring your phones to school and not to use them in the open, this logic is irrational as it tends to defy the whole purpose of having a phone. Better ways to protect yourself are:

- Not to have the most up-to-date mobiles, or palm pilots and definitely not to show off with them.
- Not to show or tell people what you have in your bag.
- Keep your money hidden in different areas of your body and clothes, so you don't have to hand it all over if you're mugged.
- Be prepared about the realities of peer violence – it happens and it may happen to you.
- Don't fall into the macho bravado of pretending it's not going to affect you or bother you if it does happen.

The latter two points are especially important because the idea that you have to fight or show guts because you're a boy can put you in more danger of being hurt.

If kids your own age are attacking you, the advice is the same as if an adult was attacking you.

1. Call for help. Look adults in the face and ask them to call the police and keep shouting until someone does.
2. Get out of danger quickly. Hand over your phone, don't fight for it and don't throw punches, especially if they out number you and are bigger and more aggressive.
3. Don't carry a weapon for your own protection. It isn't a good idea as it's likely to be turned against you in a fight, or you could hurt someone and end up being in trouble yourself.
4. Tell your parents what is happening to you, or a friend so they can help, especially if the problem is happening on the way home from school. Again don't be macho – it's braver to say you need help.

5. Get active, so you can run, and get away from potential muggers and violent gangs. Remember, there is never any shame in protecting yourself with your ability to simply move quicker than anyone else.

Sexual crimes

Less than one per cent of the crimes recorded by the police each year are of a sexual nature, though many do go unreported. While it's important to keep the risk in perspective and not let it get in the way of you leading a normal life, make sure you keep yourself safe by remembering the following:

1. The majority of abusers are known to the victim. If someone you know starts behaving in a way that gives you an odd feeling you should be wary.
2. Beware of people you befriend online.
3. Never leave a party or place with someone you have just met.
4. Always use licensed mini cabs.
5. Giving consent means you freely – without any pressure – choose to say 'Yes' to something.

Sexual assault covers more than you probably think. Any kind of intentional sexual activity and touching without your consent – which under the new Sexual Offences Act 2003 includes you being made

to touch any part of someone else's body, clothed
or unclothed, with your body or with an object – is
sexual assault. As is flashing and voyeurism (when
someone takes pleasure from watching other
people undress or other people have sex).

Remember sexual assault is never your fault, and
though you may not feel you can go to the police
it is very important to talk to someone about what
has happened as the effects are far reaching. Don't
suffer in silence see the Resources section (on page
97) for people to contact for confidential help and
advice.

Bullying

Bullying is a form of constant attack and if it's
happening to you, you need to find out how to
keep yourself safe from harm. Not sure if you're
being bullied? Well here's your checklist:

Bullying is:

Being called names.
Being harassed.
Feeling threatened.
Being teased (when it's not funny).
Being physically attacked.
Being forced to give money/do someone's work.
Having your stuff thrown about.

Being excluded.
Being pulled and pushed.
Being picked on for your religion or your race.

Like being attacked by a stranger the effects of bullying are far reaching. Bullied people often have more than cuts and bruises and many are left feeling depressed, insecure, self-hating, lonely or frightened.

"There are these boys at school who are always baiting me. Calling me a tart and basically waiting for me to go mad. One day I am worried I'll just lose it with them."

HAYLEY, 14

"These boys where I live chuck things at me when I walk past them. I am scared of them but I don't let it show."

GARY, 14

If something like this is happening to you here's how to protect yourself and stay safe.

- If someone calls you names or tries to wind you up, ignore them. If it happens in school, report them to a teacher you trust (be sure to tell the teacher what action you'd like them to take and what you don't want them to do). If it's on the way home, walk quickly and confidently and then speak to your parents or an adult you trust about it. As hard as it is not to respond remember, they are trying to get a response out of you. To stop and get into a verbal argument is to play right into their hands.

- Don't take risky short cuts to avoid bullies. It's always better to walk in places where there are lots of people and places of safety than to use an area that may be quiet but unsafe. Again if attacked on the street yell for help. Make it clear you're not friends messing around.

- On public transport, don't sit upstairs or in an empty carriage. Stay near the driver and other passengers and ask for help if trouble starts.

- If someone attacks you (hits, punches, pushes, pulls or touches you) report them at school and tell your parents. Once a bully knows he or she can get away with something physical they will keep doing it. Protect yourself by making an assertive stand against them with the help of others.

- There are three main types of bullying: physical, verbal and something known as indirect bullying. This is a form of intimidation where someone spreads nasty stories about you, turns people against you or bullies you by text, phone or email (see chapter 5). If this is happening to you, keep a diary of what happens and make sure you tell someone what's going on. Schools are required by law to protect you. If the bullying has become physical intimidation you can also get the police to step in and help.

What NOT to do in the face of danger

If you know for sure that you're being followed, stalked or someone is about to bully or intimidate you, your code should be – think about your options and then take immediate action. Panic happens to us all when we're scared (see chapter 2 for reasons why) and can often lead to bad judgement calls. Things not to do include:

1. Turning around and attacking the person you think is going to attack you.
2. Trying to fight a person coming at you – a grown adult is always going to be physically stronger than you are.
3. Screaming obscenities at the person (it will antagonise them).
4. Trying to kick a male attacker in the balls – something many people say they would do but hard to do if the attacker is faster and bigger than you are, and you're in a panic.

Instead:

- Try not to let your fear overwhelm you (keep practising the fear pyramid from chapter 2) and think about what escape action you can take. Where can you run to for safety? What adults are around who look like they could help you?

- When asking for help, don't just scream at anyone, actively look at people and ask for help. People are more likely to come to your aid if you make them realise you are asking them for help (plus it stops them assuming someone else will step in and help you).
- Your mind will always try to associate the present confrontation or scary situation with something negative from your past, perhaps a reference to an old school bully. Do your best to ignore this by focusing on the present moment. To do this – breathe! It sounds stupid but there's nothing like breathing to bring you back into the present. Plus, we tend to stop breathing or breathe very shallowly when scared and this makes our heart pound, and stops oxygen from getting to our brains.

How to get away from someone

"I'm not very fit but whenever I've been in trouble or seen it coming it's amazing how fast I have managed to run."

LEAH, 14

"I just leg it – it works every time."

MATT, 13

If you think you are being followed but aren't sure, cross the street and then immediately cross back to see if you are right. You can also stop and look in a shop window and see if the person keeps walking or stops and pretends to do something else. Then if you are sure you're being followed:

1. Head towards a public place with as many people in it as possible. Once there, phone a relative or phone the police.

2. If you think a car is following you quickly turn around and head in the opposite direction towards a public place; a car cannot turn around as easily as you can. Don't stop to give them hassle. Someone can pull you into a car faster than you think.

3. Make a note of things while they are still in your mind so that you can give details and descriptions if you need to. How does the person look, what does the person sound like? How are they dressed?

4. Even if nothing happens always tell someone about the incident, especially your parents. This is not only to put your mind at rest but also to alert people to the fact that there is someone strange about. If you and your parents think it is serious, give the police the details you have collected so they can look into it.

The worst-case scenario

Always remember: Running away (towards help and other people) is always your biggest means of defence.

Again this is because conflict puts you at risk of getting hurt. No matter how fit and strong you are it's nearly impossible to defend yourself against an adult or someone intent on hurting you. Remember it's not a case of losing face, or being cowardly but a case of escaping and protecting yourself.

When running from danger:

- Your aim is to get to the nearest place of safety.
- Avoid empty spaces where no one can come and help you.
- If you're on the road, run towards oncoming traffic and don't weave between lanes or you run the risk of being knocked over (a larger risk than you think).

- Always aim for an area where you can see people – witnesses tend to stop people from trying something violent.

Like everything in life there are always worst-case scenarios where maybe you can't run away or have been taken by surprise. But, studies show people who are passive and taken by surprise when attacked tend to get hurt just as much as those who are not. Meaning, don't give up immediately just because someone has taken you unaware.

Here are the 'dos and don'ts' of being attacked:

Do give your bag to someone who is trying to steal it. The chances of being hurt if you refuse are high. **Don't** listen to his or her threats about not telling someone. Take in as much personal information about the person as you can and pass that on to the police (it may stop someone else being mugged or hurt).

Do try to stand up to someone who is trying to carry you off. Fight back as much as possible. Your aim is to shock them in any way you can so they let you go and you can make your escape.

Don't agree to be taken somewhere else just because an attacker promises you he or she will then let you go. Never believe anything an attacker says to you.

Do work with what you have – scratching, biting, poking in the eyes and kicking all work.
Don't use a weapon. Nine times out of ten an attacker will take it off you and turn it against you.

Do give 100%. Go in with less than that and your attacker will then know they have nothing to worry about.
Don't hope the attacker will go away if you ignore them. They won't.

Do make some noise. The bigger the racket you can make, the more attention you'll attract and the less likely that someone will try something on.

Don't feel embarrassed about screaming, shouting or drawing attention to yourself. Remember, you are trying to attract attention.

Do concentrate on the person in front of you and not the image and fear they are trying to project.
Don't assume your attacker will be a man. It could be someone your age, a woman, an older person and even someone you know.

Do tell yourself that you can escape and are determined to escape or defend yourself. Think like a victim and you may be one.
Don't throw yourself out of the frying pan and into the fire. Take a calculated risk to get away, don't jump onto railway tracks or run into fast traffic just to escape from someone.

Do instil uncertainty into the person confronting you by trying to escape or defend yourself.
Don't wait for the 'right' time – there may not be a 'right' time.

Do realise you might get hurt fighting to get free from someone.
Don't let this stop you from trying.

Do work through your adrenaline surge and fear – you'll come out the other side and have moments of rational thought when you can take action.

Don't think just because you know what to do you won't feel panic. Even the most seasoned and trained fighter feels fear. It's a normal bodily response.

Do ALWAYS tell someone what has happened to you.
Don't blame yourself and keep it quiet.

Do overcome your fear of hurting the other person – remember they are hurting you and you need to get them away from you.
Don't fight back half heartedly because you're scared to do something mean to them, or because you imagine you're too small or weak to stop them.

Why you need to tell

"I never told anyone I was being bullied for months because I was so ashamed. I didn't want my parents to think I was weak and no-one liked me and I also felt like these girls were picking on me because I had done something to them. I spent the whole time feeling scared and lonely until my sister found out and told my parents. Now I realise I had nothing to feel bad about – and they were the ones who should feel ashamed."

NINA, 15

People who have
been hurt through no
fault of their own
often feel shame and
blame themselves. As
if somehow they
brought on the attack
or they should have
fought back harder.
This is a natural
response and even
though it is wrong, it
often stops people
from getting help and reporting the incident.
If you have ever been through an attack, a bullying
incident, a mugging or any sort of intimidation or
you know someone who has, it's essential to seek
help. Seeking help doesn't mean going to the police,
or being forced to face your attackers, it simply
means telling someone what has happened so you
can get some help and support.

Reasons to speak up:

1. The underlying effects of being attacked eat into
   your confidence, and can leave you feeling fearful
   and depressed for a very long time. Luckily
   there are people who can help you combat these
   feelings. People like your parents, friends, school
   counsellors, Victim Support and the police.

2. The person who attacked you may do it to someone else. In fact if he or she got away with it with you, the chances are they will try it again and put someone else through what you're experiencing.

3. Talking about what happened helps you to purge your fears and makes the future less scary. Re-living the story over and over in your head only makes you re-live the pain.

4. Speaking out will put the attack in perspective and thereby stop it from affecting you when you're out and about alone.

5. You'll see that there is life beyond what has happened. Horrible things happen and when they do we feel we will never get over them. The reality is we can and we do.

CHAPTER FIVE

Techno-safety

"I know not to give personal details to chat rooms or websites, but I was in a game group and you had to give details to get news of latest games and suddenly I started getting lots of really sick mail. I felt horrible and didn't say anything. My parents keep asking me why I have gone off the computer."

SAM, 13

You may think you're safe when using your mobile and your computer, and you are as long as you always think wisely about what personal information you're giving out to others (and this includes mailing lists). Of course, it's easy not to think about what you're saying when it involves typing or texting, but the key is — if you wouldn't say it to a stranger on the bus don't say it through your mobile or computer.

Being safe online and on your mobile means taking responsibility for your actions.

- Don't chat to strangers.
- Don't tell people where you live and what school you go too.
- Don't join groups because they say you have won a prize.
- Do tell an adult if a friend tells you they are going to meet an online friend.
- Don't send pictures of yourself over the net.
- Don't open email attachments unless they are from someone you know offline.
- Don't agree to meet someone you don't know (how do you know they are who they say they are?)

Online safety

Most people who go online have positive experiences, but like anything we do in life there are risks. The online world like the normal everyday world is made up of a large variety of people – good, bad, polite, rude, interesting and, unfortunately, exploitative. As a young person you are more at risk of the more horrible elements online simply because you are online for longer and more likely to participate in online conversations.

Online danger is often in the news. You may think you're too smart to ever be taken in by someone on the computer but it happens all the time to the smartest and brightest of people. This is why you should never underestimate the power of what's known as 'grooming'. This is where an adult spends months persuading a young person to trust them. They usually start off pretending to be someone else (usually someone your own age) and slowly reveal themselves, sowing seeds of doubt into your head about trusting other people in your life (such as your friends or parents) and at the same time reassuring you that they alone understand you. What this person is doing is isolating you from everyone else in your life but them, and then they suggest a meeting.

The good news is – you are in control. You can stop them, because with one click you are out of the conversation. If they continue to harass you on your user address (email) report them (details in Resources, page 97).

To avoid the worst from happening, think about the following safety tips when online:

• Who are you chatting to?

A person online may sound like a 15-year-old boy into Arsenal FC and pop music, but even if you have

seen a picture – how do
you know that their online
persona is real? Think
about it – you could easily
fake being a boy or girl
online, which means other
people can too. People say
all kinds of things on email
– they exaggerate, promise
things and sound funny and
witty – the reality is often
very different.

- What are you saying and telling people?

Always take responsibility for your actions. Don't
say something online that you wouldn't say to a
stranger i.e. don't flirt, be suggestive or rude just
because you think you can hide behind your
computer screen. It not only tempts someone else
to do the same but also can make a conversation
spiral out of control pretty rapidly.

- What are people saying to you?

If you feel odd about what a person is saying
don't just push it to one side. Trust your judgement
and your ability to decipher what's appropriate
behaviour and what isn't. Remember if you're too
embarrassed, scared or anxious to repeat it, it's
something to tell a trusted adult about.

• What's exploitation and what isn't?

Anything that makes you feel uncomfortable, uneasy, scared, sick or shocked is exploitative. Usually this is material of a sexual nature but it can also be violent images, suggestive emails or obscenities. If you're scared by the turn a conversation has taken or by emails you're being sent, log off and tell your parents or a trusted adult. Don't stay silent, it will just make you more fearful (see page 99 for what your parents can do).

AOLs instant safety checklist

1. When posting a profile never tell anyone online your last name, address, phone number, mobile number, password or the name of your school.
2. Don't agree to meet an online friend in real life, ever (not even with your best friend in tow).
3. Only visit moderated chat rooms – you'll be saving yourself a lot of hassle.
4. Don't click on hyperlinks and make sure you know where email files are from before you download them.
5. Tell an adult you trust if anything online makes you feel uncomfortable.

Online problems to watch out for

1. Junk email

Commonly known as spam. This is the electronic version of mail you don't want from people you don't know. Spam is a major concern for all Internet users – as junk emails may contain nasty content. Many major ISPs (Internet service providers) like AOL are committed to reducing the number of junk emails that all their members receive and have automatic filtering systems that block the majority of spam before it even reaches your mailbox (check with your ISP to see how they can help).

2. Downloading

To avoid being overloaded with spam emails never download or open any email attachments from an unknown or questionable source. Files attached to email can contain computer viruses or Trojan Horse programmes, which can compromise the security of your account.

3. Instant messaging

Instant Messaging is very popular as it enables people to communicate one-on-one and in real time. More than two billion Instant Messages are sent daily across the AOL network alone and IDC (a group of analysts who predict IT trends) claimed that in 2002 there were more than 195 million consumer Instant Messaging accounts. With online safety in mind, remind yourself that in the same way you wouldn't just strike up conversation with a stranger when walking down the street you shouldn't do the same via Instant Messenger.

4. Websites

Take responsibility for your actions online and only access age-appropriate websites. With such a variety of sites available on the Web, it's tempting to look up dodgy or even rude stuff, but remember most of these websites can log onto your email address and start sending you stuff.

5. Scams and hoaxes

Most online scams and hoaxes are easy to avoid. As a general rule of thumb, treat any unusual email you receive with the same scepticism you would treat a letter that arrives out of the blue from an unknown source. Don't click on hyperlinks or download files, don't forward the email on to other people and don't give out any personal details.

6. Chain letters

These are emails that basically promise you wealth, riches and happiness, but then ominously warn that if you don't send the email on to other people all kinds of trouble will come your way. Again like normal chain letters these letters are ridiculous and untrue, and if they upset you think how a friend would feel if you sent it to them. Don't think twice about deleting the message.

7. Attachment horrors

These are attached files that can contain pictures, images and text. If you receive one that is of a sexual nature or makes you feel sick, ill or upset tell your parents or a trusted adult immediately, so they can stop it happening again. To safeguard yourself always ensure you don't download attachments from people you don't know. If in doubt delete the email and block the address from your email account (this stops the person being able to contact you again). Check with your ISP (Internet service provider) and parents for how to do this.

8. Bullying online

Like real life bullying (see chapter 4), bullying online has the same effects. If someone is sending you hate emails threatening you by email or intimidating you with emails, keep all the evidence and take it all to a trusted adult.

Mobiles and texts

The great irony with mobile phones is on the one hand they are an essential safety item as they mean you can call for help at any time, but on the other they are pure temptation for people looking for something easy to steal. To safeguard your mobile, mobile phone provider Vodafone suggests:

- Look after your phone as you would your purse or wallet.
- Keep your phone with you at all times and never leave it unattended.
- Never have your phone visible when you're travelling.
- Don't use your phone in crowded areas where you feel unsafe.
- Despite these precautions you may be unlucky. Phones can be replaced so never put yourself in danger if confronted by someone trying to steal your phone; it's not worth it.

Another problem with mobile phone safety is bullying by phone. Studies from the children's charity NCH show that one in four people have been bullied through text messages. This is when someone calls you or sends you a text (SMS) to scare, threaten or upset you. This kind of bullying is particularly scary because the idiot doing it usually blocks his or her number so you don't know where it's coming from.

To avoid this and help yourself if it's happening to you:

- Be careful who you give your number to and insist people don't pass it on.
- If you have a blue tooth phone, switch it off in busy places where people may try to 'bluejack' you. This is where people randomly send stupid messages to people with blue tooth technology phones in busy places.
- Never reply to an abusive text or call. This doesn't mean ignore what's happening but don't engage with the bully. Save the message instead and keep it as evidence.
- If you're afraid you will accidentally erase the message, write it down along with the time it arrived and the number, if it's there.

- Contact your mobile phone network – they can help in a number of ways by barring the bully's number, helping you change numbers and even tracking down the culprit.
- Anonymous and abusive phone calls are a criminal offence under the Telecommunications Act 1984, so you're not worrying about nothing, the problem is taken seriously.

Using your mobile and texts for safety

"My phone is a godsend I am always calling my mum at midnight when I have missed the last train. She gets mad but always says she is glad I called for help. I don't know what I'd do without it."

KIMBERLEY, 15

"I used to hate my parents checking up on me all the time, but since I started texting them when I got to places and when I left, they have been cool with me. I feel less hassled and they feel less worried."

JOE, 14

Mobile phones and texting can be one of your biggest safety assets if you use them properly.

Text your parents

The charity, Milly's Fund, launched a 'Teach Your Mum to Text' campaign aimed at keeping parents in touch with their kids by phone. Milly, who was 13, disappeared on her way home from school in March 2002. Gemma (Milly's sister) started teaching her mother how to send text messages after her parents started calling her on her mobile worried about where she was. The idea behind the safety campaign is that texting is:

- A good and easy way to keep in touch with your parents.
- Discreet and less obvious than a ringing phone.
- It takes two seconds to send a 'hello' text at agreed times.
- It's easy to teach your mum how to do it.
- It's quick to pick up.
- It's a powerful weapon in the personal safety game.

Look after your friends

Finally, watch out for your mates when you're out and about. Not everyone is aware enough to think about personal safety all of the time. When you're having fun sometimes common sense takes second place and friends get tempted to do something out of character. It's easy to get pulled along by stronger personalities, and maybe even get involved in something we know is risky.

When this happens, you may need to step in, and give a strong opinion to a friend especially when he or she is about to launch themselves into a dangerous situation or do something scary. At other times you may even have to take control of a situation and say, 'Right we're getting out of here now because…' or even step back and issue an ultimatum. This isn't always the easiest thing to do. Your friends may make you feel that you're making a fuss about nothing, or that you're being a spoilsport or you may simply feel that it isn't your place to make a fuss.

However, never let other people make decisions for you – keep yourself safe by: listening to your gut instinct; staying aware of what's going on around you and putting yourself in a place of safety when you feel threatened or scared. It may not look like the coolest thing to do or feel like the bravest, but I guarantee you won't regret looking after yourself and your friends.

Resources

Safety advice and help

Milly's Fund
www.millysfund.org.uk

Suzy Lamplugh Trust
Tel: 020 8876 0305
www.suzylamplugh.org

Be Safe, Be Secure Campaign
www.homeoffice.gov.uk

Counselling help

Childline
This is the free and confidential 24-hour helpline
for children and young people in the UK.
Tel: 0800 1111
www.childline.org.uk

The Samaritans
Tel: 08457 90 90 90
www.samaritans.org

Victim Support
Tel: 0845 30 30 900
www.victimsupport.org.uk

Rape Crisis
Tel: 0115 900 3660
www.rapecrisis.org.uk

Bullying

Bullying online
www.bullying.co.uk

Kidscape
www.kidscape.org.uk

Internet

Think U Know – government advice
www.thinkuknow.co.uk

Internet safety
www.getnetwise.org

ISP (Internet Service Provider)
All online communities such as AOL have a set of
rules defining acceptable conduct, known as the
Conditions of Service (or COS). For instance, you
can report unacceptable online behaviour which
breaches COS by clicking 'Notify AOL'.

The Internet Watch Foundation hotline deals with reports of potentially illegal Internet content, go to www.iwf.org.uk

NCH
www.nchafc.org.uk/itok

Chat room advice

www.chatdanger.com

www.netaware.org

www.safekids.com

Filtering tools for the Internet

http://spam.getnetwise.org/tools/

www.kidisafe.co.uk

Sexual offences

Rape and Sexual Abuse Support Centre
Tel: 020 8683 3300
www.rasasc.org.uk
Counselling and support by telephone and post.

Survivors UK (for men and boys who have
been assaulted)
Tel: 0845 1221201
www.survivorsuk.org

Index